MW01232967

TREESⓆFHOPE

LIBRARY OF CONGRESS PUBLISHER'S CATALOGING-IN-PUBLICATION DATA

Names: Trees of Hope (Organization), author. | Escobar, Nicole, designer.

Title: *Royal parent guide: a parent's guide on sexual abuse prevention and body safety empowerment for teen girls* / written by Trees of Hope; designed by Nicole Escobar.

Description: Fort Lauderdale, FL: Trees of Hope, [2021]

Identifiers: ISBN: 978-1-7367546-5-8

Subjects: LCSH: Teenage girls--Counseling of. | Teenage girls--Sexual behavior--Counseling of. | Sex instruction--Study and teaching Parent participation. | Sexual consent--Study and teaching. | Sexual ethics for teenagers--Study and teaching. | Body image in adolescence--Study and teaching. | Date rape--Prevention--Study and teaching. | Date rape drugs--Identification Study and teaching. | Dating violence--Prevention--Study and teaching. | Online sexual predators--Identification--Study and teaching. | Sexually abused teenagers--Services for. | Date rape victims--Services for. | Victims of dating violence--Services for.

Classification: LCC: HQ27.5 .R696 2021 | DDC: 306.7/08352--dc23

Royal Parent's Guide

A PARENT'S GUIDE ON SEXUAL ABUSE PREVENTION AND BODY SAFETY EMPOWERMENT FOR TEEN GIRLS

WRITTEN BY TREES OF HOPE
DESIGNED BY NICOLE ESCOBAR

PUBLISHED BY

p. 4

The Royal Parent Guide

Being a parent involves wanting to provide the best opportunities for your child as they grow up into adults, while also protecting them from the dangers of the world. Adolescence is an exciting yet challenging time for both parents and teens. Teens are developing more independence, facing new social situations and school pressures, and discovering who they are as a person.

Adolescence is also the stage of life when your teen is most likely to experience sexual abuse. This parent guide has been specifically curated to aid you in deepening your understanding of the issue, along with developing effective communication tools to work together with your teen towards a life free from sexual abuse. Knowing the facts about sexual abuse, how it applies to everyday life, and what practical tools are helpful to strengthen vulnerabilities can have a significant impact on your power to ensure your teen's safety.

This resource contains the guidance necessary to equip you with an understanding of the ways in which everyday vulnerabilities can be manipulated by perpetrators. In addition, each topic will provide guidance on how to start sexual safety conversations with your teen. This parent guide serves as an additional prevention tool alongside *Royal*, our teenage girl prevention magazine which addresses the specific dangers of sexual abuse in everyday life and provides practical tools developed for personal safety empowerment.

We suggest that you read through *Royal* in order to understand what your teen will be learning about sexual abuse prevention and use this parent guide as a resource for developing a deeper bond with your teen through effective communication.

In *Royal*, we've asked your teen to think about the people they encounter in everyday life, what type of relationships they have, and their level of trust with those people. We encourage you to make a list of trusted people in your life and to talk about your teen's list with them. This will allow you to understand who your teen feels comfortable talking to and feels supported by, and why they chose those specific people to be within their trust circle.

When reading through this guidebook and implementing prevention practices into your family's everyday life, we encourage you to think of yourself as part of your child's armor. You are the shield that both protects them from danger and provides them with the strength and support necessary to defend themselves. Together, you and your teen will have the power of prevention.

Contents

Contents

01.

What Is Sexual Abuse?

Sexual abuse takes place any time someone engages in sexual activity with another person that is not consensual. Most people believe that sexual abuse always involves rape, but the truth is that this type of abuse comes in many forms including but not limited to rape, sexual assault, exposure, fondling, voyeurism, and commercial sexual exploitation. It includes touching and non-touching behaviors. Sometimes, sexual abuse doesn't occur between a teenager and an adult, but rather between teenagers.

As a parent, it's comfortable to believe that you know everything that is happening in your teen's life and that you have prepared them well enough so that they are never affected by sexual abuse. You've had the "sex talk" and have told them to stay away from strangers. However, the real challenge is acknowledging that sexual abuse can be perpetrated anytime, anywhere, by anyone in your life.

In this section of *Royal,* **we provided your teen with examples of Contact and Non-Contact forms of sexual abuse** so they have the knowledge to identify the different forms by which sexual abuse can be perpetrated. In addition to reading the list provided, on the next page we provided some additional behaviors to be aware of as a parent to identify a potential sexual abuse perpetrator in your teen's life.

Red Flag Behaviors To Be Aware Of

- Making others uncomfortable by ignoring emotional, physical, or social boundaries and limits.

- Teasing or belittling a teenager to pressure them into an unwanted situation or action.

- Making sexual references or telling sexual jokes when children/ teens are present.

- Exposing teens to adult sexual interactions without apparent concern.

- Having secret interactions with children or teens.

- Spending excessive time texting, emailing, or calling teens.

- Babysitting children often for free, taking teens out on special/private outings alone.

Remember that trusting your instincts is crucial for sexual abuse prevention. Remaining aware of concerning behavior and speaking up on those gut feelings can be the key difference in helping your teen live a life free from sexual abuse.

It's important to know that teens need a continuous flow of information, conversations, and engagement regarding how to protect themselves from sexual abuse. In the following sections, there will be suggestions on how to act out different scenarios that may happen in their lives and effective conversation starters. Think about the conversations you wish your parents would have had with you. Looking back, is there anything that you could have known or done to better prepare you for dealing with potentially threatening situations? This is a good starting point for mentally mapping out the type of information you want to include when talking to your teen to guide them towards becoming empowered in their personal safety.

02.

How Common Is
Sexual Violence
Among Teens?

According to RAINN, girls who are in between 16 and 19 years of age are about four times more likely to experience some form of sexual abuse than other teenage girls.

The Center for Disease Control reported that adolescent girls between 11 and 17 years of age account for 30% of females who have experienced rape.

Approximately 33% of teenage girls who have engaged in sexual activity have reported feeling pressured to do so. (Resource Sharing Project, 2011).

t's essential to acknowledge that it does not matter whether your teen attends private or public school, whether your family lives in a nice neighborhood with low crime, whether a teacher can help your teen get into the best colleges, or whether you consider your friends to be like family - sexual abuse can occur any place anytime, by anyone. For example, a participant from *Thorn*, our teenage girl healing study, shared her experience of being sexually abused by her older sister's boyfriend when she was only 13 years old. Another participant shared her story of being sexually abused during a slumber party by an older teen who was considered a family friend for years. These stories only provide a glimpse into the reality that is sexual abuse, and how individuals who you love and trust can manipulate that relationship towards sexual abuse.

Although the stories and the statistics are disheartening to hear, they are essential in understanding the severity of the threat of sexual abuse. You are taking the first step towards strengthening any vulnerabilities in your family's life. The most important thing to remember is that you and your teen have the power of prevention.

03.
What Is Consent?

G irls are going through an overwhelming number of changes during their teenage years. Going through puberty and getting their period for the first time may feel like an intimidating experience. In addition, the pressure of being popular, running in the right social circles, or wanting to fit in, along with achieving expectations of high academic achievement and extracurricular participation, can make everyday situations feel complicated. As girls begin to develop crushes and become more interested in having romantic relationships, consent becomes an extremely important aspect of their everyday life.

In *Royal,* this section includes information on the definition of consent, how to integrate consent into relationships, and how developing open and healthy communication about consent can lead them to become a more empowered woman.

We encourage you to integrate consent into your family life in order to provide a real-life example for your teen to follow. The honesty and transparency behind asking for consent and receiving consent will allow your teen to develop personal boundaries and learn how to defend those boundaries.

- Ask your teen for consent when you would like to give them a hug.

- Have your family members also ask your teen for consent when wanting a hug, a kiss on the cheek or forehead, or any touching such as a pat on the back - explain that it's a way to teach them to protect their boundaries.

- You can integrate consent in everyday aspects of your family life and use those moments to talk with your teen about different situations regarding consent.
    - For example, if your teen consents to a hug, after the hug you can ask "What should I have done if you said no to the hug?"
    - If you see a movie or television scene where two people hold hands or kiss, you can ask your teen "How did that character consent?", "How could the other character have asked for consent?"
        - You can also use moments from the media to ask about your teen's life - "Do any of your friends hold hands with each other?", "What do your friends think about kissing?", "What does hooking up mean to you?".
    - Use small moments to have these small talks about consent so that your teen feels that it is a conversation rather than a lecture.
        - Listening to your teen is the key - their perspectives may be different than yours, so making an effort to understand how they view daily life situations will help you navigate your conversations.

Teenage girls often face coercion when they are placed in uncomfortable positions in which they may feel pressured, influenced, intimidated, or manipulated into engaging in sexual activities. It's important to remind your daughter that no matter how difficult the situation might seem, she always has a choice. Remind her that someone who truly respects them as a person would not force any expectations on her. There is always a way out towards safety.

04.
Body Safety
Guidelines

Your daughter is unique. Every single thing about her belongs to her. She has her own laugh, her own way of loving others, her own body, and her own sense of self. Talk to your daughter about her attributes - What does she like about herself? Is there something she believes she does really well? What does she have the most fun doing? Learning to embrace her uniqueness will help build a foundation of confidence and self-respect; this will help strengthen vulnerabilities such as low self-esteem that predators manipulate to their advantage.

From ages 11 to 16, teen girls will have increased curiosity about their own bodies, sex, and relationships. It's normal for teens to have questions about sexual activity and wanting to experiment touching or kissing with peers of the same age. During these times of curiosity, communication is your most powerful tool as a parent. The goal is for you to be your daughter's main source of reliable information regarding sexual activity and relationships. It's okay to feel uncomfortable about the topic of your teen and sex, but remember the root of these conversations won't be based on sex, it will be based on body safety.

Teenagers may not want to speak about sex and safety with their parents due to feeling awkward or embarrassed - it is your job to break through that barrier and help them feel comfortable in speaking to you. It's important to remind yourself to remain calm when your teen approaches you with a sensitive question or shares a personal story about sexual activity. As shocking or overwhelming the situation might seem, love and support are always the most helpful reactions.

How To Show Interest In Your Daughter's Life

- Ask them about their friends - even learning their names is already a step in the right direction.

- Find out what is expected of them in school - Who is their favorite teacher? What class do they dread the most?

- Do they have a crush on anyone?

- Why do they get along with their social groups?

- If they are in a relationship, ask what their partner is like and what they like about them as a person. How do they make each other happy?

- What does your daughter feel is expected of herself?

- Use your own personal stories from when you were her age to relate to her.
  - Knowing your past experiences from adolescence may allow your teen to feel more comfortable bringing up sensitive topics and ask you questions rather than seeking information from her friends or the internet.

- Nobody is perfect - if you don't have the answer to one of her questions, acknowledge that! It's better to take some time to research and develop a helpful response, it will show that you are honest and willing to make an extra effort towards giving your teen reliable knowledge.

- Emphasize respect in everyday situations - for example knocking on doors before entering someone's room as a sign of respect, asking for consent before hugging someone because you respect them, acknowledging how certain words or actions make someone feel because you respect their emotions.
  - Using everyday situations to integrate a small reminder of the importance of respect can help your daughter understand that giving and receiving respect is one of the most important qualities of a healthy connection.
  - They should never share a special or unique part of themselves with someone who does not respect them.

p. 15

In this section of *Royal*, we have provided examples of appropriate and inappropriate touching along with everyday situations that leave teenage girls vulnerable to being sexually abused. We encourage you to study these examples in order to uphold appropriate touching amongst your family and friends, speak up whenever you witness inappropriate touching and think about any other vulnerabilities in your teen's life that may leave them at risk of experiencing sexual abuse.

This section also includes a list of practical examples of establishing and protecting boundaries for teenage girls. After reading the list provided, a good activity for you and your teen is to practice the different uncomfortable scenarios and responses. We suggest acting out each example separately on different days so that your teen remains engaged for a couple of minutes and can absorb the information without feeling overwhelmed or bored. This exercise will encourage your teen to mentally plan effective responses that protect their personal body boundaries.

05. The Grooming Process For Teens Explained

Think about all the people who are involved in your teen's life - this can include relatives, teachers, coaches, mentors, doctors, classmates, neighbors, babysitters, and anyone else that your teen may love and trust. Now, think about the fact that 93% of abuse is perpetrated by someone the victim knows. A perpetrator will groom your teen for sexual abuse through a long-term process of manipulating trust, power, isolation, and secrecy. Learning how to identify the warning signs of the grooming process and being actively engaged in your teen's life is essential for protecting your teen's virtue and safety.

This section of *Royal* provides an in-depth description of each stage of the grooming process for teens. We encourage you to read each description in this section of *Royal* to gain an understanding of the several ways by which a perpetrator will exploit your teen's vulnerabilities. To help you further strengthen your teen's armor, we have provided examples of concerning behavior along with guidance on addressing this topic with your teen.

Identify and Target

Providing effective supervision will decrease the probability that a perpetrator will target your teen for sexual abuse. Perpetrators often attempt to take advantage of teens who have low self-esteem and who seem to have weak communication bonds with parents. If you fulfill your teen's needs through providing validation, being open to listening to their troubles and questions, giving them reliable information, and prioritizing quality time; then your teen will be less likely to seek that fulfillment elsewhere.

- Try to attend every extracurricular activity, practice, and games that your teen participates in - many organizations provide several practice time options for parents with busy schedules.
  - This will show your teen that you are supportive of them, and it will also show perpetrators that you are involved in every aspect of your teen's life.
  - Conduct your own background check on any organization your teen might want to become involved in and any instructor that might come into contact with your teen.
- Be a source of encouragement rather than a source of pressure.
  - Acknowledge whenever your teen feels proud themselves or accomplishes a goal. If you notice they have something to improve on, practice that improvement with them. Working through an obstacle together will allow you to understand how they feel while preventing your teen from feeling pressured and alone. You can help them develop better study techniques - make flashcards together, work through math problems together, read their assigned books. Another idea is to have them teach you their new dance, run through lines for a play, or practice new techniques to improve their endurance or agility in their favorite sport.
- Maintaining a calm and understanding demeanor when speaking to your teen is essential for creating an open conversational bond. Reacting to your teen's honesty with love and support will encourage them to speak to you more often, rather than seek the comfort of communication with someone else.

Building Trust

Special attention and privileges may seem harmless and be perceived as providing your teen with an opportunity towards improvement or towards gaining more responsibility. In reality, a predator can be using that to develop trust and move into the next step of the grooming process towards sexual abuse.

- Has your teen been receiving special attention, private free services, or gifts from older teens or other adults in their life?
  - Perpetrators will try to fulfill any gap in your teen's life through gifts, flattery, and access to activities that may not be allowed by parents.
- Striking up a casual conversation about your teens' day on the ride home from school or practice is a good way to integrate essential questions that may provide a warning sign that your teen might be interacting with a potential predator.
- Ask what was their favorite part of the day, of an activity, or of practice? If they received a compliment or an award, what was it for? Did anyone else receive the same treatment? What makes them feel comfortable or uncomfortable in class, during an activity, or on the field?
  - Remember that it is a conversation - don't ask all the questions at once. Build communication from what your teen shares with you, not what you expect to hear from them. Allow your teen to speak their truth and really listen to their experience.

Isolation From Family And Friends

The greater the distance that a perpetrator can create between you and your teen, the greater the power and control they will have to sexually abuse them. For example, tutoring or coaching lessons should never be done in private and without the knowledge and presence of a parent. In addition, your teen should never be alone with a doctor. If you are asked to step out of the room, we encourage you to request an additional nurse to be present so that your teen remains protected.

- A major red flag is if teachers, coaches, youth leaders, and/or mentors are interacting with your teen without you knowing.
  - Establish rules of interaction with your teen and other adults in your teen's life.
    - Other adults may only contact your teen through a group text with you in it when outside of a school, mentoring, or coaching setting.

Secrecy

Addressing the difference between privacy and secrecy is key as your teen is growing into a more independent person. Here are some ways you can describe the differences between privacy and secrecy for your teen:

- Privacy comes from respect for personal boundaries. Some examples of privacy include knocking on a door before going into a room or showering and dressing in private. Privacy is about keeping yourself safe.
- Secrecy comes from being dishonest with others. Secrecy comes from a place of fear, not strength. Your teen has nothing to fear from you, so they should never feel forced to keep a secret from you. Strength comes from honesty, so if your teen is honest with you, then you will both be empowered enough to overcome any obstacle.

Continued On Next Page

The Grooming Process
Continued

Initiating Sexual Interactions

Survivors of sexual abuse have described coaches disrespecting body boundaries by physically fixing their form or helping them stretch as an excuse to inappropriately touch them. Perpetrators will also take advantage of your teen's inexperience with sexual interactions by introducing them to sexual content and touching. Let your teen know that they can speak to you about anything - you are their ally. Becoming comfortable in talking about these sensitive topics will increase the likelihood that your teen will seek primary information from you and will feel supported enough to disclose any inappropriate behavior to you.

Maintaining Control Of The Relationship

Sexual abuse is driven by a perpetrator gaining a sense of power and control over their victim. Many perpetrators will trigger a fear of parents finding out about sexual activity in order to keep teens quiet about the abuse. Empowering your teen to be brave enough to believe in their gut instincts and to feel comfortable enough to speak to you about anything in their life is a fundamental tool towards preventing sexual abuse. Here are some positive reinforcements to integrate into your everyday conversations with your teen:

- "I believe you."
- "You're the most courageous girl I've ever met."
- "Becoming more independent means believing in yourself and the power of your voice."
- "I'm always here to listen."

06.
What Is Teen Dating Violence?

Girls often have their first kiss and their first relationship during their teen years. Healthy relationships have the potential to be exciting and provide your teen with an additional source of happiness in their life. Unfortunately, approximately 1 in 9 girls experience sexual dating violence before reaching the age of 18.

This section of *Royal* provides examples of dating violence through physical, sexual, verbal, and emotional abuse. This section also includes descriptions of the different ways in which an abusive partner can manipulate your teen, practical advice on how to build a healthy relationship, and helpful reminders of self-love and empowerment. We encourage you to read this section of *Royal* and return to this parent resource for guidance on dating safety talks with your teen and how to help your teen build a standard for their own healthy relationships.

Foundation of a Healthy Relationship

A first step to take towards teen dating violence prevention is understanding your teen's view on relationships.

- What are some values you look for in a partner?

- What do you think are some characteristics of a healthy relationship?

- What's the process before getting into a relationship?
    - Here, you can use your own personal stories of your past romantic partners, or current relationship to be more relatable to your teen.
    - Remember that your teen is living in a different

world than you did when you were their age. The world of relationships is complicated - teens can go from being friends to talking to hooking up, to being exclusive, to finally being in an official relationship. Be open to learning about the experiences that your teen goes through.

Once you gain deeper insight into your teen's perspectives, you can introduce more sensitive questions to help them build a standard of safety. You can use the media and your teen's social world to your advantage in this situation - use a movie scene to identify the healthy or unhealthy characteristics of a relationship; ask about their friends and their dating habits. Here are some examples of questions to use in your talks:

- "How do you define love?" "What are some safe ways to demonstrate love?" You can even talk about different types of love such as friendship love, family love, or relationship love.

- "Are any of your friends dating?" "How do they treat each other?"

- "What do you think would be the best way to solve a problem with your romantic partner?"

- "What are some ways to establish and show respect in a relationship?"

- "How does your partner show trust and respect towards you?"
    - Trust and respect are both the bravest and strongest qualities your teen can contribute to themselves and their relationship.

- "What emotions do you hope to feel in a healthy relationship?"

- "What are some emotions that could be felt in an unhealthy relationship?"

- "How would you establish your body safety boundaries with your significant other?"
    - In building an open line of communication with your teen, you are also teaching her how to develop her own standard of healthy communication with other significant people in her life.

Warning
Signs Of Dating
Violence

1. Manipulative or possessive interactions such as your teen's partner deciding who your teen can and can't be friends with, and forcing your teen to behave in specific ways such as texting them every hour or having your teen's social media password and controlling their account and posts.

2. Changes in your teen's academic performance and/or clothing style after becoming involved in a romantic relationship.

3. Signs of depression at home and in school.

4. Risky or self-harming behaviors such as drug use, alcohol use, cutting, unsafe sex, etc.

Remember that building an open line of communication with your teen is a long-term process. Although you might want to get all the answers from them to have as much information as possible to protect them, it's better to take it one conversation at a time. Integrate one or two questions into everyday occasions so your teen feels comfortable rather than overwhelmed when speaking about sensitive topics. We encourage you to emphasize ideals of respect, love, support, and trust when speaking to your teen about healthy relationships and preventing dating violence.

07.

What Is
Online Sexual Abuse?

From school assignments and virtual classes to dating apps and social media, your teen is constantly exposed to a plethora of online content every day. This section of *Royal* defines online sexual abuse and indicates online dangers such as catfishing on dating apps, live streaming, sexting, and online harassment. Follow up with your teen regarding the safety tips listed at the end of this section in *Royal* - Why do they believe each tip is important regarding their use of technology? How does each tip help them in strengthening their armor against online sexual abuse?

A good way to become involved with your teen's online activities is by asking them to teach you how an application works and becoming knowledgeable about social media trends on Instagram and TikTok. For example, learning a viral trick or trying out trending tips can help you bond with your teen while also giving you an opportunity to learn about what they are exposed to online. Remind your teen that the same personal safety guidelines that they follow in real life should also be used in their online world.

Tips To
Decrease Online
Vulnerabilities

Establish guidelines regarding technology use. Collaborate with your teen in deciding how much screen time is allowed per day - compromise will allow them to feel that their voice is acknowledged in the household and will encourage them to follow the set guidelines.

Set age-appropriate filters on your teen's phone applications, television, computer, and other devices that connect to the internet. Many applications have digital safety features that are useful to protect your teen's privacy.

- Some features include setting the account as private instead of public, blocking location services, reporting of inappropriate content or profiles, and age restrictions.

Several types of parental monitoring software are available to aid you in expanding your ability to supervise and protect your teen from inappropriate content and dangerous online predators. Parental monitoring software provides features such as setting time limits, blocking specific application downloads, tracking multiple devices, filtering content, and providing online activity reports. Before investing, we suggest you conduct thorough research to determine which type of monitoring software best suits the needs of your family.

Help your teen understand the impact that their digital footprint can have on their future. Once your teen posts something, it will remain on the internet and become a part of their digital footprint. Deleting any type of content does not guarantee that the content will disappear.

- Go through your own old family photo albums with your teen - while you share personal stories about those pictures, emphasize how those pictures are private and special because you control who you share them with. If those pictures were posted online, anyone could have access to them forever.

Ensure that you have all of your teen's account information so that you can check up on the type of content they are posting, who is interacting with them, and what type of content they are being exposed to. It's extremely difficult to shield your teen from being exposed to inappropriate or suggestive online content. We suggest you encourage your teen to be honest with you if they do view that type of content, either by accident or due to curiosity. Treat mistakes as opportunities to learn rather than situations to punish.

As established throughout this parent guide, one of the most effective prevention tools that a parent can use is communication. There is a misconception that discourages parents from addressing sensitive topics such as sex, alcohol, and drugs because it might encourage their teen to engage in risky actions. The reality is that having constant conversations with your teen about those sensitive topics will provide them with the reliable knowledge they need in order to make informed, safe decisions in challenging situations when you are not around to guide them.

The best form of preventing drug-facilitated sexual abuse is to avoid any consumption of alcohol and drugs. However, there are still several ways by which your teen can decrease their vulnerability. Read through the descriptions of commonly used drugs, their symptoms, facing peer pressure, and how your teen can strengthen their shield against abuse in this section of *Royal*.

- Use small moments to talk to your teen about moderation. For example, if they ever eat too much and feel really full or have a stomach ache, you can use that moment to talk about how having too much of something can make them feel bad - no matter how good it tastes or how fun it is to have it.

- Give your teen information about how alcohol can affect their body.
    - There are websites that provide blood alcohol calculations based on gender and body weight - this can help your teen keep in mind how beer, wine, and hard liquor can impair their mental and body functions based on how much and how fast they consume it.

08.
The
Link Between
Drugs and
Sexual Abuse

- Help them understand that their specific body tolerance for alcohol is not the same as their friend's tolerance, so they should never feel pressured to consume the same amount of alcohol at the same pace.
- Date rape drugs can be used by anyone to perpetrate sexual abuse, even those who your teen trusts and loves.
  - Act out different dangerous scenarios where a perpetrator could slip a dangerous substance into your teen's drink - How would you decline a drink that someone else made you? What could happen if you put your cup down for a minute or have someone else hold it for you? Who would be the person you trust to have a buddy system with at a social gathering?
- Remember that your teen is living in a very different world than you were at their age. The type of peer pressure they are feeling to smoke, drink, and hook up with several peers can be overwhelming. They may feel that refusing to take part in the same social activities as their peers might make them seem less cool and alienate them from fitting in.
  - We encourage you to integrate peer pressure scenarios in your small conversations with your teen. Here are some helpful statements to tell your daughter regarding peer pressure:
    - "You are not defined by someone else's opinion."
    - "The bravest thing you can do is be yourself."
    - "Surround yourself with people who lift you up, not tear you down."

Teens may feel confused by their experience of sexual abuse because alcohol or drugs were involved. Teens may also avoid disclosing their experience of sexual abuse because they are fearful of getting into trouble since alcohol or drugs were involved. Whenever your teen is going out to a social gathering or any type of situation where alcohol or drugs might be present, we encourage you to gently let them know: "No matter what happens, no matter how bad you might think it is, I'm always here to listen".

09.

Sexual Abuse Myths

p. 28

With a plethora of information, media coverage, and public opinions about sexual abuse, it's possible to feel overwhelmed or confused about the reality of sexual abuse and how it can truly affect your teen. In this section of *Royal*, we have outlined common sexual abuse myths along with corresponding accurate facts and statistics that portray the truth about sexual abuse. We encourage you to read through the myths versus the facts and talk about the knowledge you've gained with your teen's trusted adults along with people in your trust circle. If the trusted individuals in your life and your teen's life develop a stronger understanding of sexual abuse, then you can all work together towards prevention.

p. 29

10.
Symptoms Of
Sexual Abuse

p. 30

Behavioral Symptoms Of Sexual Abuse

- Trouble focusing in school, extracurricular activities, or sports.

- Nightmares and/or sleeping issues.

- Anxiety and Depression.

- Unhealthy eating habits along with significant weight loss or weight gain.

- Changes in personality and mood such as increased anger, fear, fatigue, or insecurity. This can also include different clothing style and changes in personal expression.

- Fear of being in certain places or around certain people for unknown reasons.

- Resistance to being alone with a specific person.

- Self-harming behavior such as increased drug use, binge drinking alcohol, cutting, and running away.

- Extreme worry regarding a boyfriend's expectations and reactions.

- Exhibiting adult-like sexual behaviors.

- Withdrawal from family and friends.

Physical Symptoms Of Sexual Abuse

- Bruising or scrapes on the body.

- Pain, discoloration, bleeding, or discharge in the genitals, anus, or mouth.

- Soreness and/or difficulty walking or doing other physical activity.

- Sexually transmitted diseases.

- Pregnancy.

> "
>
> **S**exual abuse prevention includes being aware of your teen's surroundings, vulnerabilities, and potential abusers in their life. It also includes being aware of any behavioral and physical symptoms that indicate your teen may be experiencing sexual abuse. Remember that a combination of behavioral symptoms, physical symptoms, and reactions to different people and environments is a warning sign of sexual abuse.

11.
What to Do If
Your Teen Has Been Sexually Abused

Enduring the trauma of realizing that your teen has been sexually abused can bring an overwhelming wave of emotions such as shock, denial, blame, pain, grief, and frustration. It may feel like your whole world is suddenly crashing down upon you. You may ask yourself: How did I not see the warning signs? What could my teen have done to avoid this? What could I have done better to protect them from abuse?

One of the most important steps towards healing involves acknowledging the impact of sexual abuse. Remind your teen that it was not their fault, and remind yourself that it was not your fault either. Remind your teen and yourself that healing is possible and that the future is bright with hope.

In this section of *Royal*, your teen is provided with guidance on reporting sexual abuse to a trusted adult and the authorities, seeking medical attention, and seeking support during their healing journey through counseling or survivor-led healing groups. We encourage you to learn this information so you may support your teen towards their own healing journey.

In order to help guide your teen towards rebuilding trust and confidence in themselves, we encourage you to meet your teen's bravery in sharing their story with you through a loving, comforting, and supportive embrace:

- "I believe you."
- "Thank you for sharing with me."
- "It wasn't your fault."

- "You are not what happened to you."
- "We can overcome anything together."
- "You are not alone."
- "I'm here to help you in any way you need."
- "I love you."

Accepting the reality of sexual abuse can be challenging, but not impossible to overcome. As a parent, you can provide your teen with the support they need to break through from being a survivor to being a thriver.

Here at Trees of Hope, we want to help your teen overcome a life shadowed by the pain of sexual abuse through empowering their healing journey to become the bright light that will guide them towards a safe and joyful future. We encourage your teen to become involved in *Thorn*, our customized healing program for teenage girls who have experienced sexual abuse.

p. 33

Made in the USA
Middletown, DE
08 May 2022

65480610R00022